Turning Back to Her Love Pages

Turning Back to Her Love Pages

Poems by

Judy Lorenzen

© 2025 Judy Lorenzen. All rights reserved.
This material may not be reproduced in any form, published,
reprinted, recorded, performed, broadcast,
rewritten, or redistributed without
the explicit permission of Judy Lorenzen.
All such actions are strictly prohibited by law.

Cover design by Shay Culligan
Cover image by Gonzalo Facello on Unsplash
Author photo by Steve Lorenzen

ISBN: 978-1-63980-757-4

Kelsay Books
502 South 1040 East, A-119
American Fork, Utah 84003
Kelsaybooks.com

*This book of poetry is dedicated to my mom and dad,
though these poems will never capture the love and gratitude
my sisters and I hold in our hearts for our parents.*

Acknowledgments

Thank you to the following publications, in which versions of these poems previously appeared:

Autumn Sky Poetry DAILY: "Sometimes I Get Lost in Memory"
Jama's Alphabet Soup: "Cinnamon"
Nebraska Life: "The Arrival of the Hummingbirds"
Plainsongs: "My Father's Grapevine"
Quill & Parchment: "What Mother Taught Me," "Mother Always Chose Joy"
Silver Birch Press: "JC Super Salt," "Your Signature"
Sparks of Calliope: "Fog"
Times of Singing: "Autumn Theatre"
Verse-Virtual: "That Autumn Day"
Your Daily Poem: "My Father's Love"

Contents

I. Second Chances

Turning Back to Her Love Pages   15

II. Portraits of Mother

Squash Blossom   19
I Remember   20
Mother Listened When to Go   22
What Mother Taught Me   23
Remembering Mother When Leaves Burn Red   25
Her Simple Pleasures   27
Mother Takes a Poetry Workshop with My Sister and Me   28
That Autumn Day   30
And She Prayed   32
Small Things   34
Their Garden   36
Autumn Theatre   37
The Bougainvillea   38
Marigolds   40
June Moon Shining on Clematises   41
Lauren's Letter   42
September and I Think of You   44
Perseid Shower   46
Autumn's Good-bye   48
Mother Always Chose Joy   50
Mom's Nicknames   51
Cinnamon   53
Your Signature   54

III. Portraits of Father

What The Great Depression Taught My Father	57
All That My Father's Father Taught Him and Gave Him	59
What Brought Him Back?	60
And Then There Were Horses	61
He Learned He Really Could Be Anything He Wanted to Be	62
SPAM, Not the Fake Email, the Fake Meat	63
George Jones Really Loved My Father	64
Fog	66
The Wood Ducks	68
Father Today	71
Sometimes I Get Lost in Memory	72
JC Super Salt	74
My Father's Grapevine	76
My Father's Loves	77
Father	78
The Things of October	79
Myosotis	81
Becoming Father	83
My Father's Life	84

IV. Love Lives On

Psalms, Songs, Rain, Streets	87
Arrival of the Hummingbirds	94
Until Death Would They Part—But Not Even Then	96

I. Second Chances

Turning Back to Her Love Pages

How do I honor the memory
of my mother and father,
whose love story began in 1949,
when they married after six weeks of meeting,
her, a high school graduate, waiting tables
at the Compass Room in Lincoln,
him, a young WW II vet with a GED,
the cook at the Compass,
both from poor families—
a baby girl nine months later,
with six more girls to follow
throughout the next nine years,
one, Jill, severely disabled?
If love could die from troubles,
the heart-framed mirrors of their hearts for each other
would have shattered.
But she loved him with a rare love that always
reflected back a beautiful image of the one it was set on.
He learned in time how much he loved her.
Her love, he said, was spelled out all over
the pages of his life from 19 on.
And what is love anyway?
A commitment to stay—no matter what?
"Please, Sugar,
turn back to your love pages
that you wrote for me," he told her
at the breaking point of sorrows.
He wanted her, he wanted her love back,
he wanted the curls back
that she wore around her face just for him,
he wanted to see, again, those truthful blue eyes
that he loved to look into,

to have, again, those sweet lips
talk softly to him, laugh with him,
to have those arms of comfort around him, again,
to have her heart that loved him so deeply,
to be the object of that love,
he wanted for her
to turn back to her love pages
and write the end of their story
from that point on in love
because love, as she taught him,
keeps no record of wrongs and never fails—
and she did.

II. Portraits of Mother

Squash Blossom

Holding Mother's hand,
we walked to the garbage hole
behind the evergreen trees on our farm.
In her threadbare green housedress
and worn tennies,
she pitched trash
into the midst of burnt black cans,
rusted car parts,
half-burnt milk cartons,
a green vine thriving—
I've learned the way life is:
when all seems lost,
in the middle of the mess and busted frames—
a squash blossom,
big, orange, green tendrils crawling everywhere,
promising future fruit.
I remember
a season later,
brisk autumn air,
skipping to the garbage hole,
Mother picking the squash,
me—carrying it to the house,
supper, the sweetest orange mash, blossoming.

I Remember

watching Mother take care of Jill,
though I was three, and Jill, six.
Jill would cry and Mother would hold her,
stroke her hair, talk lovingly to her
until her pain settled down.
Then, I remember, one day,
Jill was gone,
and there was no more crying in the house.
I remember the first time we visited Jill
in the Beatrice State Home,
and I think back to the day Mother told me
that the doctors insisted she place Jill there
because the staff was equipped to give Jill
the kind of care she needed—and after all—
they reminded Mother—she had three daughters younger
than Jill who needed her attention,
and so did the older three.
I remember Mother's blue eyes crying as she told me
she did not want to give Jill up.
Those days must have been dark, dark days for her—
impossible days with that decision in front of her.
And I think of how she loved Jill with all of her heart,
and when I had my own children,
I thought of what it must have been like for her
to watch six of us grow healthy and strong,
while Jill struggled to breathe and eat.
I remember how Mother's love and care,
how her sadness and tears for Jill's life,

washed over us like gentle spring rains,
the rains she loved so much—
that promised new life to the grasses and trees—
how they left drops of hope in her heart for Jill
who was born into her life with such profound limits.

Mother Listened When to Go

When you hear the sound of marching in the tops of the balsam trees, you must act quickly because that is the sign that the Lord has gone out in front of you . . .
—2 Samuel 5:24

Something told my mother's heart
it wasn't time to go,
though the fields lay browning
a small voice whispered, "No."

The leaves in red attire
cautioned a coming frost,
and still the small voice whispered,
"Your hope is real, not lost."

The chilly nights were stirring
coyotes and field mice,
creatures that remembered
the coming of the ice.

The summer birds were leaving.
It was time for them to fly.
As they winged across the heavens,
she listened to their cries.

Still listening for the marching
and watching this earth's show,
she learned in every season,
there's a time to stay and go.

Then with the springtime blossoms
and the return of wild geese,
she heard at last the marching
in the tops of balsam trees.

What Mother Taught Me

It was the last night at our house on the hill
in Malcolm, Nebraska, the place my nine-year-old heart loved.
Dad's truck was loaded and ready to leave in the morning—
we girls would ride in the old white station wagon with Mom.
That evening, I sat under the mulberry tree
at the end of the sidewalk and cried,
looking up through my tears at the stars,
a hundred thousand points of light in the soft violet sky.
Mother found me and asked what was wrong.
"Look at my trees I love,
smell the fragrance of these green grasses,
listen to the crickets' last song for me,
and look, look at those stars—
I'm losing everything!"
My kitty seemed to understand and comforted me,
bumping her head on my chin to pet me and herself.
We were taking her with us,
along with our German shepherd.
I remember Mom saying,
"We'll take your sky with us.
Who could leave this weight of starry glory behind?
Tomorrow night, you'll see."
And my stars were there the next night,
radiating like her promise over our tiny house.
But that same night, my kitty left
to return 99 miles to Malcolm all by herself,
and I cried, surely, as many tears as stars in the sky.

We found my kitty, now a cat, the next spring
when we returned to the old house
to drive by and see it—there she was.
"Leave her here," Mom said.
She was right—I couldn't take her home with me,
not because she had turned a little wild,
but because I knew exactly how she felt.
I wanted to stay, too.
That day, Mother taught me
how to let my wounds become my radiance
as she had done so beautifully her whole life.

Remembering Mother When Leaves Burn Red

My mother taught my sisters and me constantly—
how to read with her old King James Bible,
how to write before we went to school,
all about the seasonal flowers, trees (she loved the flowers and
    trees) and their life cycles,
the birds and their songs (she loved the birds and their songs),
types of weather and clouds (she loved thunder and lightning).
Though we were poor, she was rich in knowledge—
we were wealthy in mother.
When she taught, love flourished in her every word—
her patience in answering our questions,
her encouragement for us to ask them,
her soft answers—
her life was an example of love for us.
Though she loved all of nature and saw the beauty of each season,
we girls knew that fall was her favorite time of year—
she loved autumn trees, their colorful leaves, their brilliant story
    telling ways—

and she died in October, her favorite month.
She would have loved the red leaves that October of her death—
they were more vibrant than they had ever been.
She had told us never to snuff out autumn's fires—
let them turn to embers, smolder, and rekindle.

The other day driving home, I passed a fire bush
and thought of mother reading the burning bush story
to us in our childhood.
I remember marveling that God called out to Moses
from that fiery bush.
As a child, I couldn't wait to encounter my first burning bush,
to talk to God and thank Him for my mother
and to see why He and the bush didn't burn up—
the unburnt bush that was burning and speaking.
Mother taught us to listen,
to hear what trees and bushes were saying,
and I learned that all of nature talks—
it has its own language,
pouring forth speech continually.
Elizabeth Barrett Browning wrote
how crammed earth was with heaven—
for all of those who have eyes to see.
Mother taught us to take off our sandals.

Her Simple Pleasures

On early summer mornings especially,
when life was greening and blooming again,
she loved sitting on her pergola-covered patio
and breathing in the air that was sweet and so full of birdsong—
the coos, calls, cheerful chirping, trills, the melodies—
like my older three sisters,
years ago, rehearsing their trio
prior to their high-school choir concerts.
The birds loved Mother's huge maple in the backyard,
building their nests in it and foraging insects on its bark,
providing all they needed in their carefree world,
while they offered song.
Mother loved watching these winged artists fly in and take off,
and hearing them sing, like my sisters,
a soprano, first alto, and second alto, harmonizing.
Jamey, Jackie, and Joy'd start off
on one single note for the first line,
"I believe for every drop of rain that falls,
a flower grows . . ." and Joy, second alto,
took that "ows" on grows, down a scale of notes
that sounded sublime.
"Sing it out, Joy," Mom'd say.
Under the bird-drenched morning skies,
she'd linger, often cracking the sliding-glass door open
throughout the day to hear what song was in the air.
Sometimes, I'd hear her in the kitchen singing
with the birds or a memory.

Mother Takes a Poetry Workshop with My Sister and Me

They creep upon us, those times we'll never forget,
like when I was talking to my mother
about my Fall Poetry Workshop that I was taking—
and she started quoting John Neihardt's "Easter,"
about the northbound Wonder bringing back the goose and crane
and those majestic words about the geese being
prophetic sons of thunder—apostles of the rain.
The poem was beautiful, and I was astounded
that out of my mother poured this powerful poem
she had memorized in grade school.
Her ability to remember dates of wars and quotable quotes
always impressed me as her memory was photographic.
Then I learned that she remembered all the grammar rules
from elementary school and how to apply them correctly.
She could diagram sentences and identify all the parts of speech.
Not only could she recite Neihardt's poems,
but all of the poems she had learned in her youth.
She knew writers and poets, their genres and literary periods,
so I invited her to come to the Summer Poetry Workshop—
which happened to be about Neihardt—with my sister and me.
"Yes!" she said, and I picked up her *Black Elk Speaks,*
A Cycle of the West, and *Lyrics*
and Dramatic Poems of John G. Neihardt.
At 56, she was so excited to attend a poetry class,
and my sister and I were thrilled to attend a class with our mother.

The first day was long and filled with history and readings.
Plus, we were up early to drive an hour to the college.
When the poetry reading began in early afternoon,
I saw Mother's head bobbing up and down—
the poems were so rich,
I knew she was nodding, "Yes" to the speaker,
but, no . . . soon, I heard Mother snoring.
My sister looked at me wide-eyed and smiled.
We knew she was tired . . .
All I could think about were those certain students who,
right at the riveting, critical points in literature, fell asleep.
"Who can hold the whole audience
after the first 30 minutes or so?"
my sister whispered in my ear,
"She can recite all of these poems by heart—let her sleep."
I learned more than beautiful poetry
and fascinating history that day—
when kids fall asleep in class,
it isn't about how engaging the lesson is, but their lives,
and, my mother, though sleepy, was an excellent student
who received an A.

That Autumn Day

There was something about that October day,
that earthy scent in the air,
those golden rays beaming down in columns,
that stayed with me as Mom
and I watched the combine in the field.

She had come for a short visit,
and we walked out and stood by the fence line.
Grasshoppers hopped all over the tall dry weeds near the fence.

We watched the tall cornstalks coming down
and waved to Sam as he whirred past us in the John Deere—
I held up his brown bag lunch,
letting him know to stop next round.

After handing off his lunch,
Mom and I walked the farm and talked.
She told stories of her childhood days and the effects
of The Great Depression on her life
as the sun rays crowned her head

in golden light. Big fluffy clouds took turns
rolling past the sun. She looked like a beautiful painting
from the Renaissance era.

By the end of the day, our hair was full of autumn gusts
and my mind, of amazement of all she'd been through—
now these memories return each autumn

as colorful and vivid as the red apples on my tree. The tree
that was standing there 25 years ago—overflowing with fruit.
She took apples home to bake Dad a pie.

Like the season's ending, on goes time, so comes death.
Today the October sky is heavy gray
but the fields and geese are still singing earth's refrain,

"Time for harvest. Time to leave."
And I sit here with this knowledge that Mother's planting,
kernels of love in the soil of our hearts,
produced a harvest a hundredfold.

And She Prayed

Mother wanted someone to pray with her,
but my sisters were either gone or too busy working,
and so she prayed alone—but kept asking,
so I said yes
and learned she was a powerhouse prayer warrior.
We prayed in her room with the big map of the world
across one wall,
and she prayed, then, for years for my sisters
and their spouses finding their way,
and making good choices,
that they'd never be
destitute in faith,
for their children
that they would spared from years
in the wilderness—troubles,
any of the worldly temptations—drugs, sex, greed—
that would seduce them.
She was an old mother praying and praying
for her children and her children's children,
about the fires they would go through.
And when she finished with our family,
she prayed for her friends, their families,
and her neighbors,
and then she prayed for people groups—
according to the map on the wall,
and her prayers were not a simple sentence
but heartfelt paragraphs and essays
always spoken in tears and love,
and I wasn't sure what her biggest asset was—
her faith, love, or patience.
I began to understand that verse
that a day is like a thousand years . . .

and I would add,
an hour like a hundred,
but what I wouldn't give
to be back in her presence
peeking through the slit of one eye
at her tears falling into her lap
and hearing her sweet requests ascend.

Small Things

Long into the green days of May,
when buds have blossomed
into red peonies, pink roses,
and purple zinnias and every leaf unfurled,
so long into life and its lessons,
I remember my mother saying never
to worry about the small things in life—
those little things, she said,
were really meant to shape us,
to help us make something beautiful of our lives.
She pointed to the hummingbirds
that had just arrived in her garden,
their emerald green capes, their dazzling red throats,
flittering from flower to flower,
threading their needles and sewing reminders in the air
of their uniqueness.
Small worries will rob you of living and blind you
to the radiance all around you, she said.
Pulling down the pine branch,
she pointed to
the thimble-sized nest
in the fork of two branches.
Something hidden and beautiful is about to happen.
These little birds know how to take care of their own,
making their nests of twigs,
leaf parts and spider silk, so the nest will
stretch so the tiny babes have room to grow—
she said—
little worries will take care of themselves
if you let them. Oh, they may flash here,
dart there, quick stop, and zoom back in—
they may come back at the same time

every year. What you must do is go on living,
be faithful in the small things in your life, she said,
and be like these tiny green glitterers
that love to make their homes
in quiet secluded gardens
where living takes place.

Their Garden

When I saw them in their garden,
together, in their older years,
working, bent over,
sunlight through clouds, angel-like,
shining down on them,
I was struck by a sense
that I never understood love before
and by a desire to have more time with them.
I realized the swiftness of time—
and wished I could name this unexplainable feeling inside of me.
Was it their age that brought it out? Their garden?
Most days, she'd be amidst radiance—her deep pink dahlias,
red, yellow, pink and orange tulips, and
gold marigolds.
He'd be weeding his zucchinis,
cucumbers, tomatoes, and peas,
his coffee and garden tools beside the grape trellis.
If she caught sight of me,
she'd wave, smile,
and come to greet me and talk.
If not, I'd watch the two of them for a while,
thinking about how good the simple life is,
how forgiveness magnifies love,
and how overcoming life troubles
creates a grand entrance
to a beautiful garden.

Autumn Theatre

If Mother were still alive,
she'd call this unfolding each day
Song of Solomon's lyric love:
yellow sun caressing
sumac, elm, cottonwood, maple
greening to gold, brown, red,
singing up brome, cattails, milkweed,
yellow goats beard sending off giant parachutes:
September's verse.
Deeper golds and oranges to October's scenes
pumpkins, cornfields.
As dragonflies and swallows dip and dive in low blue air,
red-winged black bird sits on the telephone wire flicking her tail.

Wild, this show is wild in love with its players—
leaves chattering performance praise
until curtain falls
bare
under harvest moon.
November's arms
bowing to December's finale.
"Encore"—Mother would shout—"encore."

The Bougainvillea

Like the red bougainvillea's beauty
decorating the pergola outside the sliding glass door,
rich and flourishing on hot summer afternoons,
inspiring those in its presence the way that only beauty can,
Mother knew how to comfort us
by listening for hours at her kitchen table,
her blue eyes gazing at the troubled soul,
her ears attentive to every word.
Even though I knew after her hours of listening to me
her words would be, "Everything will be okay,"
I still needed to talk to her.
I still needed to hear her say them.
Few flowers could withstand such heat—
and grow, bloom and thrive hardily
in severe droughts like my mother had.
Her encouragement, never quenched,
always produced in her advice-seeker,
a profuse replica of strength to overcome troubles.
Her hope never faded, even after hearing about infidelities,
financial problems, or serious illnesses
that threatened family members' lives.
Her gentle words were a flowering force,
influencing the courses of our lives,
teaching us how to make bad situations better.

My sister in Arizona sent my other sisters and me
a picture of her gorgeous bougainvillea,
lying on her patio in a huge shattered pot.
I know what my mother would have said,
"You can restore that bougainvillea
to its former glory and beyond.
Repot it now,
and wait until it takes off
and throws a floral festival
on your patio again."

I realized on seeing that photo,
I had taken on my mother's responses to life—
to see the beauty in the brokenness,
and all that could possibly come from it.

Marigolds

with a line from Robert Frost

Late spring and these hardy marigolds
are in full bloom, composing their own
yellow and orange notes of garden music,
and I can't help but think of Mother
and how she loved these flowers best of all. She loved
how the marigold was a companion plant to her
vegetables and fruits, protecting them from root knot nematodes,
underground mosquitoes and aboveground rabbits. All the pennies
she saved in buying marigold seeds showed up in the beautiful
gold, copper and brass jewels these flowers brought to her summer
and autumn garden, lavish riches she said.
She sang in her garden—
her voice carried in through the open windows of the house,
reminding us daughters how she could not carry a tune—
yet her lyrics were sweet songs of strength
composed from her hard years of life.
It has been twenty years since I've heard her melody,
but every spring when the marigolds sing,
I hear her songs and remember her faithful companionship,
knowing that *nothing gold can stay.*

June Moon Shining on Clematises

The purple clematises, a hue deeper than the violet sky tonight,
run along the trellis and through the iron fence
like fallen stars on a green velvety background.
The full moon rises alone in a stunning appearance,
as a few stars twinkle off in the distance. This is the way
Mother was, the center of attention, and didn't try to be—
just shining her light on our problems in simple,
yet profound ways.
We all wanted her ear and her wisdom,
which felt as ancient as the solar system.
Her gravitational grip of love on us
moved us like the ocean tides, higher and higher.
The moon, even with its scarred craters, is beautiful,
and her many sorrows had carved out
the loveliness of her character, too.
I remember the first time I read
that the moon is moving away from us,
and one day, we will have it no longer.
I was sad.
The day I saw the light going out of her eyes,
I knew. Many full moons have come and gone
since her leaving, but tonight,
the moonlight on the clematises
whispers of the way she lived her life,
blooming profusely, fragrant and strong,
naturally adding beauty to this life.

Lauren's Letter

is the only keepsake from Mother's last days that I kept
as a reminder of the way I wanted to live till I died.
Lauren's voice, so loving towards Mom,
gave witness to the mother she had been to me
and the faithful friend Mother had been to others.
Her letter arrived two days before Mother's death,
Many times you have crossed my mind,
and the memories have been good.
I stop in stillness and listen carefully
to Lauren's sweet voice,
When I saw a tiny red Bible by the checkout at the counter
at Chapel Books the other day, I smiled and thought
of you. Then yesterday at Bible study, I heard your name spoken
across the table. I tuned in and heard you were in a battle
with cancer, another teaching ground on faith,
not one we get to choose.
I marvel at Lauren's tender knowledge of Mom,
knowing that those around her were always learning
important life lessons from her words and actions.
I sat wondering what you were teaching those around you.
I wish I were one of your students as I always
received from you. And my mother was teaching
my sisters and I how to die.
Lauren's next words resounded in my mind,
We have always missed you at Bible study—
do you have the strength to come visit?
She had no strength and was moving into the comatose phase
and mottling, like October's leaves out her hospital window.
The diabetes, cancer, blindness, and heart failure
were bringing her life to an its end.
Lauren's hope and encouragement to Mother was like my own—
a persuasion to her to live,

We have all tasted sorrow and persevered so far.
I hear myself saying, "Please, Mom, don't die. I need you."
But Mother could not persevere, dying October 3rd.
In my world of sorrow,
Lauren's words added such beauty,
meaning and comfort,
I framed them and hung them on my wall
for the love letter that they were
not only to my mother but to me.

September and I Think of You

I love these late September days,
fields stand crisp, golden brown;
days, warm—
all that is good
wraps 'round me like a prayer
from Mother's lips

late September,
my thoughts migrate—
like these geese lamenting loudly—
across a vast blue chasm of years,
grief calling—
what I'd give to sit, talk with you again, Mother,
you taught me to love this brilliant song of life—

so I sit under this big blue expanse, deep in thought
now beholding the magic of geese migration—
sojourners of the heavens,
caught up in the splendor, the sorrow of this day,
sumac reddens, milkweed flies,
"Your daughter, Jill, a great love, sorrow in your life;
disabled, bed-ridden—in pain,
caused you to seek answers—
the answer caused your heart to sing songs sweeter
than these birds' songs,
when you found it—
you never did quit singing—
Did I say thank you for the sweet, sweet song you gave me,
sweetest song I've ever heard?"
the last few cries of the geese in the distance—
just passing through, like you, Mother, like Jill—just passing
   through

tonight under this plum-colored sky,
stars scatter golden stardust in their spheres,
cicadas sing their songs in Forte,
I think of you—and how you taught me to love all that is about me.

Perseid Shower

Sorrow came for me
I went for solitude—
You were dying, Mother.
Evening, I strolled down late summer,
the trees had begun to turn.
What a show this earth performs
with the seasons of its year dying—
and living again—
In the midst of sorrow
autumn orange unfolds
leaves, wings unfurl.

From the peripheral edge
a shower, brilliant white lights celebrate
splashing heavens.
What is this paean of praise
that will not let me be sad?
Shooting stars
across night sky.

Last night as I lay by you,
put my face next to yours,
kissing it for possibly the last time,
"In all things give praise"—
in such a time as this?
Tonight you answer:
Death is the seed to life.
The way you live, Perseid—
a dying to yourself everyday
nourished and illuminated another,
shimmering tail,
glorious realms.

You are between two worlds—
my interplanetary rock,
burning up in atmosphere
bathing this world in beauty.
You were always dying, Mother—
Always.

Autumn's Good-bye

It's late October
when Autumn makes good on her promises:
chilly nights,
crickets' songs from fields gone gold—
when leaves glow red on maples.
It's an old promise Autumn keeps,
like an old woman repeating herself,
hair gone white as winter snows
mottled hands now folded as she speaks
on the threshold of another world.

Your beauty is beholding, Mother—
in the late Autumn of your life,
before Winter.
You tell me you are going blind
and will not get to enjoy
golds and reds much longer.
I tell you not to say these things;
I cannot bear to hear them.
You say I must be prepared.

Your words changed—
they form wearily
on withered mouth,
spoken with such tenderness—eternity.
Golds, so much golder,
dearer to you now—
if that be possible, you say.
You talk of your family
you will soon be leaving.
You talk of your Jesus
you will soon be with.
You talk of this Autumn you love—
You say good-bye.

Mother Always Chose Joy

As autumn's beauty diminished
with stacks of brown sheaves
golden leaf by leaf,
the sun left earlier each day—
Mother began her watch
for the Harris's sparrows' flight
immigrating in the dark of night
to winter in her spruces.
Little brown birds, no words
but full of song
and wisdom to build their nests
on the side of the spruce
out of prevailing winds.
Three single same-note refrains
they'd sing in the coldest winter terrain.

Mom's Nicknames

Dad called her Sugar and Honey,
because of her attitude and spirit—
and because—
he became addicted to her.
He called her Hot Rod—
her heavy foot on the gas pedal
accidently running over a pet or two—
trying to help her not feel so bad about the pets.
He called her Chiquita,
a secret name between the two of them.
He had a few other terms of endearment for her,
but Sugar was his mainstay,
the spoonful of "White Gold" that made any bitter medicine
go down.
And she was sweet, terribly sweet,
so sweet that her pancreas could not produce
enough insulin to rid her body of the sugar
that caused her diabetes, heart problems, and eventual blindness
    and cancer.
After her first heart attack,
her life became shots and pills, every morning,
finger sticks, a shot in the stomach and heart pills by mouth,
yet her joy was not diminished, nor was she discouraged.
She knew life was worth living, and love, worth giving,
and she was going to love us until the day she died.
If, as she used to tell us,
we, in our inner being, just
become more and more of what we are
as we get older, then she was honey, as Dad called her—
the sweetest food here on earth,
made by bees from the nectar of beautiful flowers.
My sisters and I always find

when we talk about our mother,
the conversation always goes back to love and goodness.
Sugar was a good nickname for her—
she left us so many sweet memories.

Cinnamon

with a line from William Butler Yeats

Where goes the memory wandering
but to the house of my childhood
to smell the sweet aroma
of Mother's baking goods.
Where her kneading hands are covered
in butter or in flour
where the crimson spice's fragrance
hangs in the air for hours.
And there is nothing better
than in her presence here,
to see her face, feel her embrace,
I feel the welling tear.
The loaves of bread and rolls dark red,
were love that served the child,
where time is gone and memory lives
my mind rests for a while.
I didn't know how fast time passed,
holding her cinnamon-scented hand,
For the world's more full of weeping than I could understand.

Your Signature

I saw your signature today
on a yellowed birthday card
that had slipped out of my card box
on the dresser and fallen
between the dresser and wall.
I shook off the dust
and recognized your loop
on the L of your name
and the slant of your cursive.
As I read your words,
from decades gone by,
your voice was alive on the page.
You told me how blessed you were
that I was your daughter
and how you hoped
I had the best birthday yet.
I heard and felt your love for me
that flowed from your pen,
which was from your heart
and written all over my life.
You always said words mattered, Mother,
and you were right.
You signed off, "Love you forever, Mom."
What is love that it lives on
after death?
What are words
that they are alive
expressing the longings of the heart,
even holding the power
of the universe in them?

III. Portraits of Father

What The Great Depression Taught My Father

be grateful for the job you have—
never assume you'll always have it
never assume you will have a home tomorrow
be grateful if you have a roof over your head
shut the lights off when you leave the room
know that all work is honorable
get rid of any pride you have
know you are entitled to nothing
don't feel bad if you drop out of school to support your mother
be proud of your GED when you get it
don't be surprised if your life changes drastically
in a minute's time
know how to find edible food in garbage dumpsters
by grocery stores and restaurants
share with the animals that are there scavenging with you
grow your own food
be frugal, never cheap
don't borrow money
know a good deal when you see one
learn to barter
never trade silk for calico
waste nothing
use everything you have
wash and reuse plastic wrap and utensils
wash and reuse aluminum foil
buy off-brand products when you have the money
buy only what you need
use only what you need
prepare enough for everyone
always serve the best of what you have
be sure the animals are fed
be generous to those in need

love your family—they are all you have
don't worry
look at the birds that never complain about their daily menu
soar
and never give up

All That My Father's Father Taught Him and Gave Him

He'd tell the story of learning who his father was—
he was a lonely child
walking down a dusty road,
kicking a can,
on his way home from school,
a black car pulling up next to him,
a window rolling down,
a man with olive skin, thick glasses and thicker accent
asking him his name.
"Jimmie Baccacus," he answered.
"No, you're not!" the old Greek demanded.
"You are Jimmie Catholos. Be right here next Friday,
same time, with your report card."
The window rolled up like
a rip sown up in the womb of the universe
in his bizarre new world
as the man in the car pulled away.
Little Jimmie showed up the following week
as directed—with his report card,
Spiro pulled up, took the report card, checked it over,
handed it back, told him, again,
"You are Jimmie Catholos," and pulled off.
Years would pass before he saw his father again,
the man whose image and likeness he was created in,
the man who taught him what a father should be.

What Brought Him Back?

Was it the picture of the seven sweet little faces
who desperately needed to know him?
Was it remembering the fragrance in the wind on the farm
when the wildflowers were blooming?
Was it the guilt that struck like blight on the blossoms
making it too hard to cure?
Was it having the foresight of the bitter fruits that would come
from the pleasures he had planted?
Was it the love of a woman
who would not stop believing in him?
Was it a vow he had spoken and committed to
years earlier?
Was it the moon watching him, night after night,
as he was making his decision?

And Then There Were Horses

Moving to Grand Island,
occasionally Dad took us girls to Kuesters Lake
to swim, while he watched the horses
run in the pasture next to the lake,
his hands propped on a post, knee on a fence board,
just watching, living his dream
of watching horses run.
And the horses ran,
often up to greet him
because they had learned
he had a sweet surprise for them,
hiding in his pockets.
I'd watch him stroke their great heads
talk to them, and offer them the sugar cubes,
which he kept in the pickup glove compartment
to fill his pockets with.
I swore those horses understood and talked back to him,
shimmying their flanks, neighing,
throwing their heads back, manes flying,
thanking him for the love,
a nose on his neck, snorting.
There was something in their prancing, an uneasiness,
that he had once felt, too, and loved them all the more for it,
that wildness, that he had let go of,
hot-blooded thoroughbreds, agile and spirited,
running fast in the race of life
that he no longer competed in
and had learned to be completely content—
no more inward pressure,
the foot to the girth to increase speed,
but a nickering, the sweet greeting
to loved ones at home.

He Learned He Really Could Be Anything He Wanted to Be

My dad was a scrappy kid
who gained wisdom in childhood
as severe poverty shaped his life,
taught him resourcefulness—
his first job as a child,
a crier at funerals.
When the neighbor boy
shoved a stick in his eye and he lost his sight,
he did not cry.
He became skilled at living life
from what he observed in other people's lives,
and even with only one eye,
he picked up the smallest details.
He learned to never complain,
and he grew up never feeling sorry for himself.
Years later, when he needed, he put on the white coat
of Dr. Van Horn
to sign the physical fitness forms that needed to be completed,
delighted to save the charges, no insurance—money in his pocket.
He sutured his own deep cuts with a needle and thread,
pulled his own teeth with pliers, and removed his own moles.
He appreciated being Phil Pheagel, Attorney-at-Law,
when he needed to fill out legal documents with legalese
and could have continued on ad infinitum.
He said Phil's attorney fees were exactly what he could afford.
Poverty taught him more than education ever could—
he learned to survive and was never a victim.
He learned, like his grade school teacher said,
he really could be anything he wanted to be.

SPAM, Not the Fake Email, the Fake Meat

There is a strange phenomenon, a nostalgia,
that happens to most people as they age.
They begin to long for the food of their youth,
no matter how grotesque—
the bologna, Vienna sausage, or canned sardines—
those foods that can only ensure that life is pleasureless.
I watched my dad crave and eat SPAM,
the food of his military service years,
Depression food from WW II.
Stationed in Hawaii, he ate it daily,
and I'm sure it was delicious to a young man,
who as a little boy rarely ever had a good meal—
and never meat.
Decades later, when he hungered for it,
he'd buy a few cans,
fry it, and make SPAM sandwiches.
It was a shiny slimy rubber rectangle—
Something Posing As Meat.
But who am I to criticize this edible brick
that needs no refrigeration
when it was credited as one reason
for winning World War II?
When I see a can of SPAM,
I can see my father, with two SPAM sandwiches
on a plate, green onions extend the bread,
mustard is visible, and he is sitting at the kitchen table
in silence, eating.
It becomes clear to me now,
why this man never ever complained
about anything in his life.

George Jones Really Loved My Father

My father did grow on people—
as he eventually did me.
He nicknamed my sisters and me
(he called me mosquito—
said he couldn't get rid of me,
and I buzzed in his ear),
my friends who came over,
my sisters' friends who came over—
anyone visiting the house . . .
I'm sure he became famous, locally,
for his unusual names for people
and for his delivery of what he said to them.
Even the neighborhood animals loved my father
because he fed all of them,
whether they had eaten at their own homes or not.
He didn't want any person or animal to be hungry.
As he filled his bird and squirrel feeders and the cat dishes,
he'd ask, "Well, what's on the menu for today?"
Animals knew when feeding hour started at his house.

I screamed late one evening at Mom and Dad's house
when I saw a creature with a scary white face
staring in at me through the glass-sliding door.
"Don't frighten George Jones," Dad said.
"He's busking again for food. He's here
to eat and then sing his latest song for me."
My father got up from the table,
put George's supper together and took it out to him
as George waited patiently, lovingly even, by the door.

"Well, hello, George, how's that new song comin'—
you gonna sing it for me tonight?"
I heard my father say as he stood there
talking to George Jones as George ate.
Then I heard my father singing honky tonk-like.
Soon Dad said, "Okay, I'll see ya tomorrow."

When he came back in, he put George's dish in the sink,
"Well, his new song is good, but it isn't quite as good as
'When the Grass Grows Over Me,'" Dad said
and sat back down at the table to visit.

Fog

A thick fog rolled in this morning,
and it's just one of those days
when clouds of memories come in
and eventually move way, as one
picture comes clearly into focus—
now I see my father sitting
in the living-room chair
after cooking in a hot kitchen
all morning and afternoon long
at The Platter on Interstate 80—
his eyes, closed,
his feet and legs aching.
Ronnie Milsap's "Smoky Mountain Rain"
plays in the background,
and I hear my father's voice,
"I've had a change of dreams,
I'm comin' home . . ."
I am moved by hearing his voice again
and realize that he was singing from a place
of deep understanding of the song—
the rain, the regret, the homesickness,
the "doing everything I can to get back, but
no one will let me in"—
and for the first time,
I see him.
He harmonizes with Ronnie
and the memory is sweet,
and just like the rain in the song
and the tears
the singer has to wipe back from his eyes,
I'd give anything
to see my father again,

a man whose love
I rejected most of my life
when the fog of resentment obscured my perspective—
then I took his love for granted
like he owed it to me.
But death and memory offer
the sorrows of hindsight,
the blessing of clear vision.
Now I see everything,
and what I see
is all that I failed at,
and what I remember
is goodness,
and the only thing I feel
is mountains of love.

The Wood Ducks

I never understood my father
or realized what a rare man
he was, until one late summer morning
on my walk. One of the first times, I was missing him
and thinking about his most unusual ways
of referencing life as he saw it—
his blind eye, "a front headlight that was out"
or his broken legs as his "dented hubcaps"—
My mother I had adored,
my father, I had not.
Deep in thought as I walked the road,
I reached the bridge over Silver Creek, and there,
where a mallard couple came every summer,
swam two wood ducks—
Startled to see them
at their first appearance ever,
I walked closer very quietly to watch them—
mainly him—
gracefully swimming,
their boxed heads moving
back and forth as they glided forward.
They were a beautiful sight—
the drake was stunning.
And her beauty was comparable,
but he had my attention.
His black cheeks with white stripes
along his neck extending intricately up each cheek,
looked like someone had carefully painted him.
My father's words, too,
were painted all over my life, so colorful.
They set him apart
from any other person I knew.

He told me of the neighbor lady's
heart disease as "her transmission's going out."
And the man down the street
with mental problems
"was slipping a clutch,"
his co-worker,
who couldn't get rid of his fever,
"had an overheated radiator."
My friend asked me one day,
What is your father even talking about?
If his words weren't car metaphors,
they were cooking verbs resulting in different dishes,
the languages of his life.

My father was like that wood duck—
captivating in this silent scenery—
with his red eyes and bill,
his metallic purplish-green plumage on his head and crest,
his yellow patch at the base of his bill,
his dark red chest and rump,
but his drab yellow side with black and white stripes at the edges
and white belly
reminded me of my father in his work clothes.
He wore his old white button-up-the-front cook shirt,
black pants,
and old worn-out black shoes
that made my five sisters and me cry
when we saw them
after his funeral,
sitting in the spot
where he always took them off.

What a palette of colors, the wood duck,
his blackish tail and back,
with his black and blue wings.
So, also, my father, the Greek,
loud in his voice,
wild in his hand gestures,
with everybody around
staring at him.

I didn't see or appreciate
his uniqueness then.
Now, I clearly see his distinctiveness,
the beautiful character he was.

Father Today

It has been
seventeen years since you died,
and you were right—
the world went on,
even though I did not want it to.
Yet, the sun comes up every morning,
and now,
the dawn is peeking
through my window.
In her silken slippers, she slides long
and quietly along the floor
bringing in the light.
She is as silent
as my thoughts
this morning—of you.

Still, darkness
surrounds me.
She is crowding it out,
so I can no longer linger
in this sweet memory
of when you were alive.

Sometimes I Get Lost in Memory

like the one of Dad making dolmathes
for the last time, his taking the fresh grape leaves
from his vine,
washing, then blanching them.
Rinsing the rice in the colander,
he sautéed the olive oil and chopped onions
until translucent, making me think
of the need to be transparent with the ones
I love and tell them before I can't. Carefully,
he added the rice and beef
and sautéed a minute longer.
When the aroma made my stomach
growl, it was time for two cups of warm water and lemon juice
to simmer for seven minutes
until the rice had absorbed the water,
then his own special season salt and herbs, his secret ingredients.
Something of the tremors in his hands made me think
about life, and I wanted to tell him I loved him,
and that love, not only food, keeps a family alive,
but my pride silenced me.
Next, he layered the bottom of our largest pot
with vine leaves and started rolling the dolmadakia.
The rolling was the hardest part
for his shaking hands.
One leaf at a time, shiny side down,
he added the filling, then folded the lower
section of the leaf over the filling, tightly
bundling them in the pot. He placed each stuffed
leaf folded side down—to the top. Pride can ruin
everything, a whole pot of Greek cuisine or someone's future.
Drizzling the dolmathes with the rest of the olive oil,
lemon juice, and secret ingredients, he poured

in enough water to just cover them and placed
an inverted plate over the top.
The waiting began—40 minutes,
then another 30 to cool down.
I wished I would have asked him questions,
and not just any questions,
important questions
like *how hard was your childhood*
growing up in a cardboard box in shantytown
in the winters? or why didn't you leave us?
No. No. I wish I would have said,
"Thank you for the dolmathes
that you made just for me. I love them,"
but pride at that time was too hard for me to swallow—
now, it just eats me up.

JC Super Salt

Sprinkling JC Super Salt
on my salad,
I think of my sister Joy's love
for my father—
he had survived
The Great Depression,
poverty, near starvation,
several stepdads,
WW II military service—
the odds—
and become a chef.
And I think of my father,
Jimmie Catholos,
who had learned the secrets
of surviving, then thriving—
a man, who in his hungry years
learned to turn a stone
into a delicious soup,
to make flavorful broths
out of meat bones,
using every herb,
every vegetable leaf,
of produce he could find,
producing a meal,
tasting of the old country.
He had secret herbs
he had blended together
throughout these years,
the most delicious briny mixture.
And Joy, always
with a heart for Dad's past
and a business head

for what was delicious,
had his secret ingredients manufactured,
naming it after him, JC Super Salt,
and placed in stores—
to his great surprise,
a gift of love,
pouring her perfume out
on the one she loved.
And JC Super Salt
made everything better—
no matter what it was sprinkled on,
his gift of love to his daughters and customers.

Still we love it on our salads most—
with each bite, Greece comes alive
and we hear the music
and see the Sirtaki
and feel our father's love again.

My Father's Grapevine

My father's grapevine sparkles
with hundreds of grape clusters
plump, purple,
with leaves, vines
traveling through this lattice—
this violet-haloed liana
reminds me each fall
of the chalice
he had to drink.
Planting the young vine after
Grand Island's '81 tornadoes—
he bought Mom this house—
their former house destroyed.
Many an afternoon,
Father could be seen
slightly bent, weeding,
caretaking,
while shafts of glory
spilled gold—
on this servant of flowers, fruits,
and birds of the air—
and filled his garden.
These grapes, now, are as sweet
as the shaking hands
that planted them.

Memories of him come
when the vine is dressed
in autumn hues, golden haze,
and I find myself
having to let go all over again.

My Father's Loves

his love of his Greek language and phrases,
"Se agapo," "Eureka," and "Opa,"
his *agapi* for life,
his *agapi* for family,
his love of the old country, Sparta,
his great gratitude for surviving starvation in his childhood
in shantytown by the Missouri River,
his love for playing his Floyd Cramer,
Ray Charles, and Ronnie Milsap albums,
his love of gardening season—planting seeds each year,
watching the earth nurse her babies—the blossoming and growth,
his love of weeding and the full fruits of his labor,
his love of his beautiful grape vine in July
and August trellising the arch,
his admiration for his pink and purple cosmos that lined the border,
his love of his green peppers, cantaloupes, and onions,
his love of his tomato plants, the crowning glory of his garden,
lush, overflowing, vibrant red laced in deep green—
and oh, those tomatoes,
red heart-shaped fruit, delicious and so good for me—
in all his Greek dishes and salads.
His love beyond his lifetime—*agape,*
alive, unconditional, knowing no time or boundaries,
that holds me now in this sweet memory.

Father

You were silent
those October days
like late hush
around your garden
in its autumn-orange sound.

So many things I didn't realize.
How you carried such pain in your eyes,
as I wouldn't let you live down your past.
You loved that thrush's song,
said that there was no lovelier melody
with its undercurrent.
You were right, so right.
so happy when she built her nest
in the bushes by your garden.

If I could do things differently—
I would.
Memories of you come now
in evening's light
as I walk your garden
alone.
Telling you I'm sorry,
over and over now.

The Things of October

I knew she wouldn't make it,
each day shorter,
mottled leaves first fell
from Dad's huge oak,
September's dirge
gave October's golden fields
she wouldn't see—this time.
How she adored autumn's dress, glorious,
reminiscent of something long forgotten—
she would say.
She passed with October.

The next two springs,
he replanted her garden.
When October came,
he'd sit at the kitchen table,
look out sliding-glass doors
over her marigolds,
pink, purple cosmos.
He'd tell her childhood
marigold story—
little girl born during
The Depression,
Brownville, Nebraska,
knew there was a God
when she crushed
a marigold, smelled it,
glimpsed other realms—

to any listener,
hand raised in air
veined to bone
a leaf turning,
shaking.
"I should have recognized signs."
He passed with October.

Her tall orange marigolds
stand frost hardy;
leaves fragrant, air bittersweet.
God of joy and sorrow
has left me orphaned
on this October day.

Myosotis

Outside my window this morning,
the forget-me-nots have blossomed
a heavenly sky blue,
as blue as the robin's egg
that must have fallen from its nest last night
and lies forgotten beneath the pine branch,
which would have broken my father's heart.
He grew so tender the older he got, loving all of nature,
especially the world of small creatures in his garden,
too busy and amazing to ever forget—
the ant carrying its morsel of food to its hill,
a mound of spilled pepper,
the spider climbing up the strands of its large web
on the grape trellis, a geometry lesson for the day,
the mouse scurrying to escape Father's sight,
crossing his vision in his one good eye,
not a floater—but a friend to remove,
the earthworms in the dirt,
plowing away through the ground, aerators for the soil.
"Don't despise the small things of this world,"
he'd say. "They have their place here, too."
In his garden, he was careful to take care
not to interrupt the small bug life going on—
watching for any chewing or destroying of his plants.
"No insignificant small thing," he'd say,
"See this seed?"
He marveled that a handful of seeds
produced his huge, lush garden
that could feed the whole neighborhood
and surrounding wildlife.
His vegetables and fruits
were equally as beautiful as his flowers.

He loved his little blue forget-me-nots, though,
the cry of his whole life—
a little boy who had been forgotten,
locked in a basement one time for five days without food,
many times, having to fend for himself.
He grew hardy, survived,
unwanted or unwelcomed, boy or man,
and learned the hard lessons of life.
Dying and being assessed to be released from the hospital,
he told the doctor he would not need help—
his daughters would take care of him—
he would not be forgotten
at the end of his life.
I remember how Joy and Jo
took such loving care of him.
I look at the little egg, alone,
its blueness shining out on the vast green,
knowing that my good intentions
of placing it back in the nest
is the worst thing to do, so I leave it
and walk on to the forget-me-nots
to enjoy their beauty
and empty myself
of this great sadness
I feel this morning
of all that has passed.

Becoming Father

Many of my memories of you—
are you, late in your life,
in your beautiful garden in the backyard,
where the birds of the air,
the butterflies and insects of the grasses
loved that garden as much as you did.
When the grapevines bloomed
in those short couple of days of their process,
your real work began.
But the fragrances that drifted
once the blossoms showed their petals,
soaked the air with the sweetness of life,
and, you, there, were drunk on the elixir of happiness
of planting, caretaking, and reaping.
Your garden looked like a well-loved garden.
On the stone by the one end of the trellis
sat your big glass mug full of cold black coffee
that kept you working all afternoon.
I remember watching you
through the kitchen window,
the sun shining down on you,
turning your light smooth Greek skin
into your dark Mediterranean roots,
roots I didn't come to understand
until it was almost too late.
I remember thinking
after life pruned away your wildness
how wonderful it was
to watch you become the father
you always wanted to be.
I remember thinking about
how sweet life could be.

My Father's Life

My father's life and death
was an antimetabole,
a type of chiasmus.
terms rooted in the Greek,
for the repetition of words in successive
clauses but used in transposed order—
Socrates, examined his life and wrote
antimetaboles, "Eat to live, do not live to eat"—
a turning about in the opposite direction.
Both definitions were true of my father's life.
My father came into this world
living the first decade or so of his life
constantly hungry and did eat to live
when he could find food. His lack of food
surely influenced his becoming a chef,
when he lived to feed others.
But his life also turned in the opposite
direction he started out in,
a little boy, without anyone really to depend on—
then as a man with a family,
he lived away from his family
then he could not live without his family.
From lost in a world without love
to loved in a lost world—
he lived to love.
He came into the world hungry,
he died starving,
the large tumor in his esophagus
blocking any food from passing.

IV. Love Lives On

Psalms, Songs, Rain, Streets

We sit at the kitchen table, 4237 Pennsylvania Avenue,
Grand Island, Nebraska—when was the last time?
"Oh Lord, you know when I rise and when I sit . . ."
This morning's bacon lingers,
rain, thunder, lightning,
old photos we gather from Father's boxes
neatly stacked in hallway closet,
holding these moments of time in our hands—
how strange that pictures meant the most to Dad.
Faint Brut rises from stained photo paper.
We study black and white ancestors' faces:
a family trip to Beatrice to visit Jill,
perched on the hood, our old white station wagon,
trees cast shadows on faces.
Jackie, with her mother-cut crooked bangs
stuck her tongue out at the camera.
Jamey shook her motherly finger at us.
A picture-covered table—"Look at this, look at that,"
Dobie Gray singing salvation's song,
about looking for light in pouring rain . . .
You sing with him, hand me . . . pictures of our dogs.
Bent over laughing, I cannot catch my breath, swirling
back to yesteryear—the day that we danced with our dogs.
Sherman Street—warm December day—school break,
neighborhood kids sitting on the tailgate,
short shorts, sleeveless shirts, barefoot, thongs,
Dad's '67 metallic gold Dodge pickup.
The forbidden music—Creedence Clearwater Revival—
loud, cranked up from inside the house, windows open.
Charles, Nancy, the twins Pam . . . Doug, Betsy, Steve
Donni, Brad, Ricky, Vicki, Janelle singing
"Down on the Corner."

Gone, those days, Mom and Dad at work.
Bummer, Cokey, and Cindy hostile dancers in 1969
that softly bit our hands.
We gripped their paws, and their little legs stepped back and forth.
When the dance was over, they came back for more.
I sang with Marvin Gaye,
"I Ain't Got Time to Think About Money."
The radio played on; we danced, I sang.
Cokey, shaggy tan coat, big eyes,
ears that pointed straight up to Jesus.
Bummer like an overgrown firedog—
white with black spots, one big black spot over his left eye.
He didn't dance well, but, Jonna, you, tried, and he growled.
He turned out to be a real bum, but you loved him anyway.
You cried when Mom said you had to get rid of him;
he ripped up Mom's new floral couch—
tore down the curtains—huge scratches on the stereo.
He knocked over plants, broke their pots!
The farmer Cablanski came to get him.
Bummer looked through the back window at us—
you stood in that misty morning, tears . . . waving.

Cindy, black with white splotches on her coat,
like someone dropped a paint can,
hit her tongue with reverse, black spots,
wagged her tail, kissed my face to dance with me.
I danced; she danced, and I sang to my dog.

That day of the neighborhood jamboree talent show,
Jamey, Jackie and Joy imitated The Supremes
in "Reflections."
Jackie held a stick as her microphone,
as Jamey and Joy harmonized the backup,
swinging their hips, in step, each soulful beat
like Motown metronomes.

Charles made bunny ears behind Betsy's head.
Betsy slapped Charles, then ran home and cried.
Like a kid at the fair pulling a reluctant calf,
Nancy pulled Charles by the ear all the way home.
Mom pulled in the drive; kids ran and hid.
Mom's arms around the six of us
in front of the yellow brick road sidewalk.
We were caught, her love forgiving—

Vacation Bible School at our house,
Cindy, Betsy, Charles, Nancy, and I,
listening to the green felt-board story,
Adam, Eve, the tree, and the snake in the garden,
Mother's eyes full of wonder teaching us.
"Jesus loves me, this I know, for the Bible tells me so . . ."

Judy with Steve—blue-eyed, blonde-haired farm boy.
Prom 1974. The Black Max Ford Fairlane.
4319 Claussen Road, Mom's dream home.
Northwest High School, tickets glued underneath photo,
our song by the Spinners, "Could It Be I'm Falling in Love?"
Graduation Day, Mom and I, 1974,
Mom, UNK nursing cap, top of her class,
I, Northwest High School, diploma in hand.

"Nurse Ratched in the family now," Dad said.
Mom laughing her belly whopper, "Oh, Jimmie, stop!"
November 2, 1975, Jill's funeral day,
Grand Island Cemetery, a tent,
rain the day she was born, rain the day she died,
"All of my days were written and ordained . . ."
The family gathered for Jill's burial,
"Sit in birth order," Dad said: Jamey, Jackie, Joy,
Jonna, Judy, and Jo—we are singing,
"When peace like a river attendeth my way . . ."
The thunder echoes time to go home: Central City.
Mike, from Mike and the Mechanics, singing
about all the things he didn't get to tell his father,
M Road lined with sumac, plums,
mud grips my tires. I slide in the drive
through this floodgate of memories.
Oh, Mom, I find myself talking to you,
looking at these captured times,
hear you sing your favorite hymns—off key.
And I wonder—
was I good daughter?
Regrets pour in.
Your love demonstrated each day,
how the laws of mathematics do break down concerning love:
You did give all of your love to each one of us girls.
Lady Liberty loved huddling masses.
You helped immigrants with language, letters, life.
My Mother Theresa, Grand-Island mother
loved the female inmates, taught them of Christ.

You taught me to love the Bible,
taught me it was thunder, lightning
in my hands and heart.
Now when George Beverly Shay's songs play, I hear you.
When Billy Graham's crusades are on, I see your smile.

When I see the pink and purple sunsets
all over the heavens, I wonder,
What are you doing up there so colorful?
What's it like being with Jesus?
What do the stars look like
from that side of heaven?
Are you glad Dad
is finally there with you?
Dad missed you so much.
A young boy in an old man's skin,
planted your cosmos, tomatoes,
talked with you every day for his day's direction,
said your address changed,
but you lived in his heart.
Do you miss us?
Looking at these photos of you,
I am homesick now.
The heavens roar; the rain comes.
Across the sky, horses' hooves thunder
and memories, like fillies stride my mind:
a strong man who could not be harnessed—
Father—with a Winston between his fingers, curls,
hanging in the air above his head like a devilish halo.
His thoroughbreds galloped in green pastures,
Repeat Performance, Two Dollar Bill, Princess Again.

Keusters Lake, a sunny Sunday afternoon
jumping off the dock in our red bikinis,
Jackie dunking Joy in the roped off section,
water splashing, cool breezes, dry shivers,
hot dogs roasting on a little fire on the beach—
Duke, Dad's dog, swam across the shore, tongue out,
1972, the year his mare broke her neck.
I hear Dad singing Ray Charles' "I Can't Stop Loving You."

Now, I feel time like the brush of your horses' manes
flying over the years in a race to the line.
Oh, Dad,
if I could turn back time, enter these pictures,
I would love you better.
That line from Mike and the Mechanics haunts me
about wishing I would have told you in your living years.
I wouldn't have held the past against you—
I remember the day I saw how sick you were.
From that day, I could not forgive myself.
Thin, unable to sit at the table and talk,
we sat in the living room,
you in the cushioned chair,
and for the first time,
I had hearing ears,
learned about your life at shantytown—
South Sioux City to the riverbank,
reach the Filly Milk sign,
your house the Burma Shave sign.
I learned how you learned who your father was,
what it was like to be a little boy
whose stepfathers didn't like him,
to grow up during The Depression,
hungry, collecting soft fruit in dumpsters.

You received the highest score for your GED,
Pacific Division Air Transport Command,
Hickam Field in Hawaii,
so much about you in a little bit of time,
and I was sorry I had been bitter,
sorry I had wasted time,
sorry that I didn't love you.
What a strange pair, my parents—until later years.
She loved him "good"—
he loved her.

Arrival of the Hummingbirds

Mother and Father loved these days
admiring winter's close, awaiting spring—
two children of The Great Depression
who never got over being grateful—
their huge maple tree out back, budding,
filled with bird feeders
for birds and squirrels—always full.
She'd tell me of the robins
hopping from green tuft to tuff, looking for worms,
to feed their babes in their nests,
and the waiting little yellow beaks wide open
that she could see—
hungry to grow up, she said,
and participate in this wild and wonderful life.
Life is busy in spring, she'd say.
Dad, farmer at heart, chef by trade,
loved the deep rich soil in his garden,
Nebraska's sweet dirt, he called it—
produces the best tomatoes
and lushest grapevines and grapes, he'd say,
with longing for the vineyards of Greece in his voice.
Mother couldn't wait for her beard tongue to bloom
in late April and her brilliant trumpet vine a little later.
She readied her red hummingbird feeders for the garden—
awaiting the flying jewels' return.
How she loved their ruby throats and emerald capes.
She'd start her watch in late April, early May—
because she knew hummingbirds remembered where
the sweetest flowers and feeders were—and returned.
There is a sweetness to this life they loved
that they never got enough of.

Dad's rescue cats walking figure eights around his legs
as he stood to gaze over his work in the garden for the day,
or sitting in his lap in the evenings, meowing at him silently,
looking drowsily into his eyes, telling him, time to eat.

The mind, like the hummingbirds,
always remembers the sweetest of loves
and returns to those memories
that grow lovelier each year.

Until Death Would They Part—But Not Even Then

How did my parents' marriage make it,
two incredibly different people—she, faith, he, hustle?
With 45 percent of marriages ending in divorce,
(career choices, parenting differences,
division of household labor, relationships with family,
relationships with friends, finances, and health),
they did not end as a statistic. Amazing.
After their arguments,
she'd read the Psalms and respond peacefully.
It wouldn't be long,
he'd call her Chiquita or Nurse Ratched,
and she'd be laughing again,
but sometimes when he really made her mad,
quietness lingered in the house a few days
before her laughter returned.
Reading the Psalms for the first time,
I realized some of them are prayers for God
to break the teeth
or arm of the opposition,
which made me smile—
someone else felt this way!
Was she imagining him with broken teeth?

My sister and I visited their graves the other day.
We couldn't help but think about
how much they loved each other,
marveling that death could never erase their love—
there it was written in stone—
nor could it make it die
as our eyes were overflowing with it.

About the Author

Judy Lorenzen is a poet, writer, and teaching artist. She is widely published in literary magazines, journals, anthologies, calendars, newspapers, and on websites. Her education includes a Doctorate of English, Composition and Rhetoric, December 2016, University of Nebraska at Lincoln; Master of Art in Creative Writing, May 2008, University of Nebraska at Kearney; Doctorate of Theology, May 2000, Andersonville Theological Seminary; Master of Science in Community Counseling, May 1998, University of Nebraska at Kearney; and a Bachelor of Arts in English, Emphasis in Writing, Philosophy Minor, May 1995, University of Nebraska at Kearney.

www.ingramcontent.com/pod-product-compliance
Lightning Source LLC
Chambersburg PA
CBHW030908170426
43193CB00009BA/779